MW00332689

Chinese
VECTOR MOTIFS

By Alan Weller.
Designed by Joel Waldrep.

Chinese Vector Motifs is a new work, first published by Dover Publications, Inc., in 2010.

The CD-ROM file names correspond to the images in the book. All of the artwork stored on the CD-ROM can be imported directly into a wide range of design and word-processing programs on either Windows or Macintosh platforms. In order to take full advantage of the unique capabilities of the vector format images you will need a vector-editing program such as Adobe Illustrator or CorelDRAW. As a bonus, we have included the freeware vector editor Inkscape on this CD. For more information, see the Read Me! file in the Inkscape folder on the CD. For the most up-to-date information about using the image files on this CD, please visit www.doverpublications.com/991105.

ISBN 10: 0-486-99110-5
ISBN 13: 978-0-486-99110-8

Manufactured in the United States by Courier Corporation
99110501
www.doverpublications.com

001

002

003

004

005

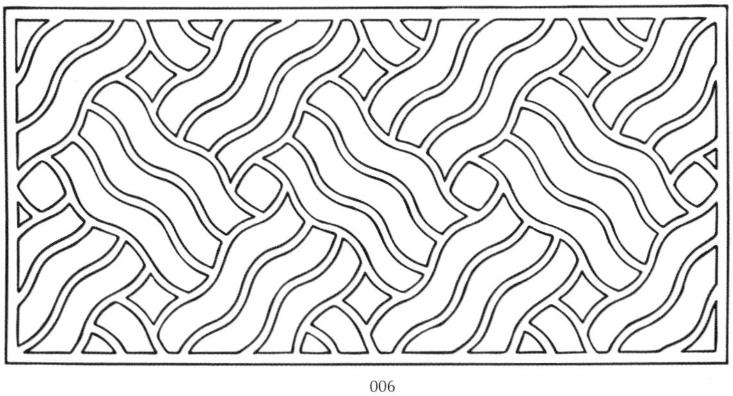

006

007

008

009

010

011

012

013

014

015

016

017

018

019

020

021

022

023

024

025

026

027

028

029

030

031

032

033

034

035

036

037

038

039

040

041

042

043

044

045

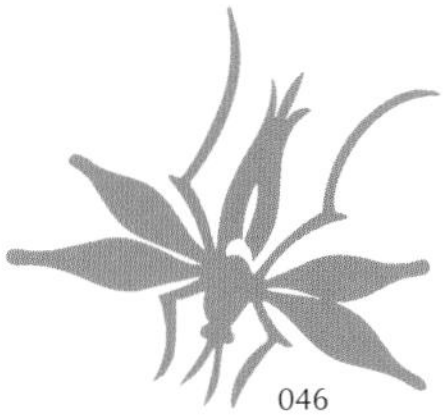

046

047

048

049

050

051

052

053

054

055

056

057

058

060

059

061

063

062

065

064

066

067

068

069

070

071

072

073

074

075

076

077

078

079

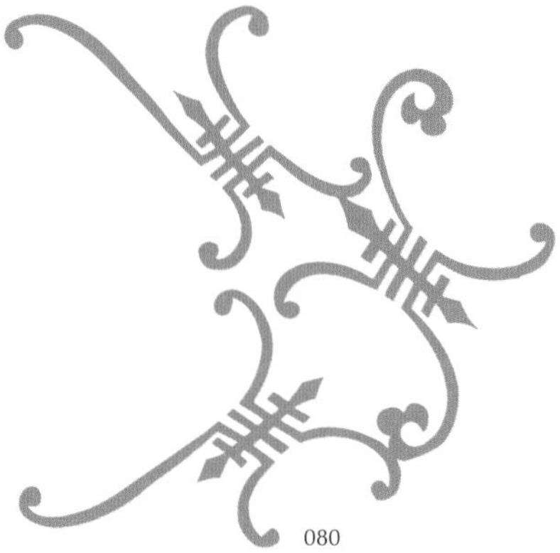

080

081

082

083

084

085

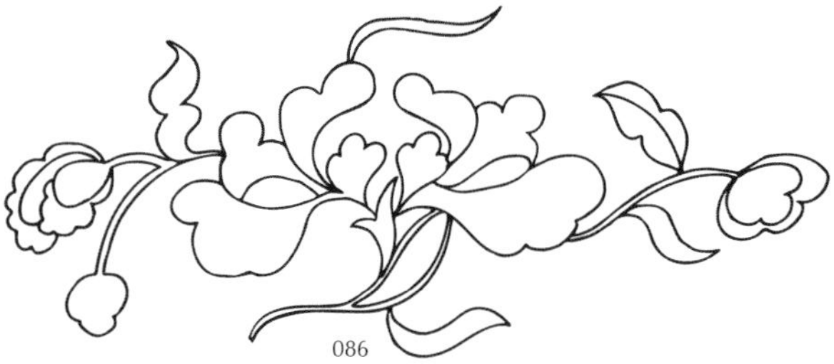
086

087

088

089

090

091

092

093

094

095

096

097

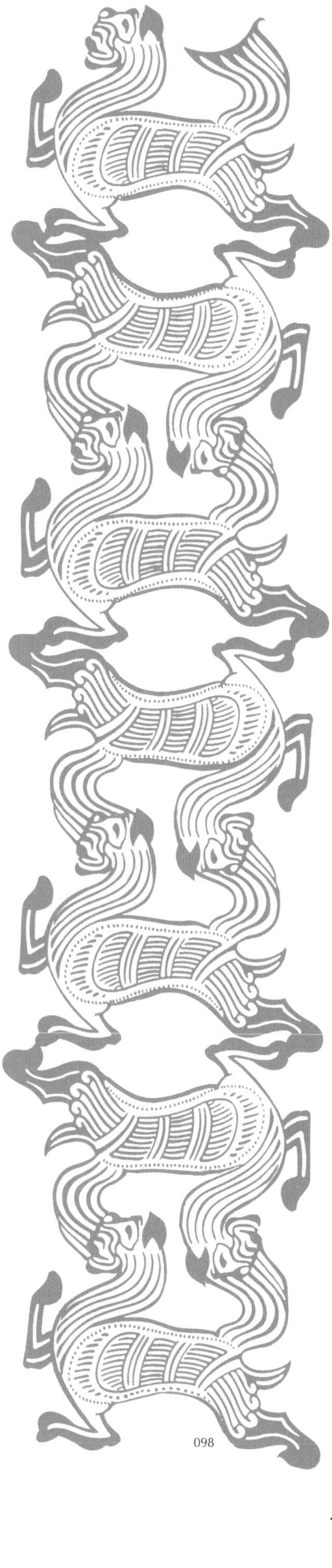
098

099

100

101

102

103

104

105

106

107

108

109

110

111

112

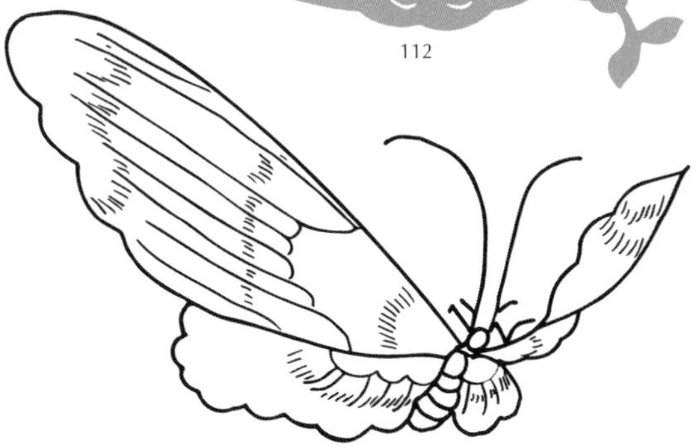

113

114

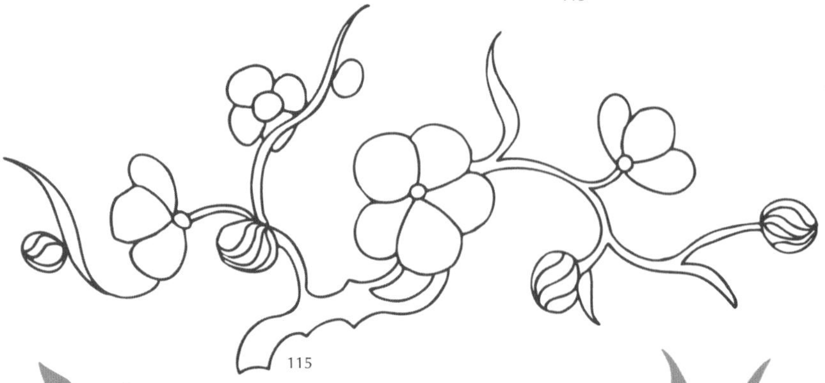

115

116

117

118

119

120

121

122

123

124

125

126

127

128

129

130

131

132

133

134

135

136

137

138

139

140

141

142

143

144

145

146

147

148

149

150

151

152

153

154

155

156

157

158

159

160

161

162

163

164

165

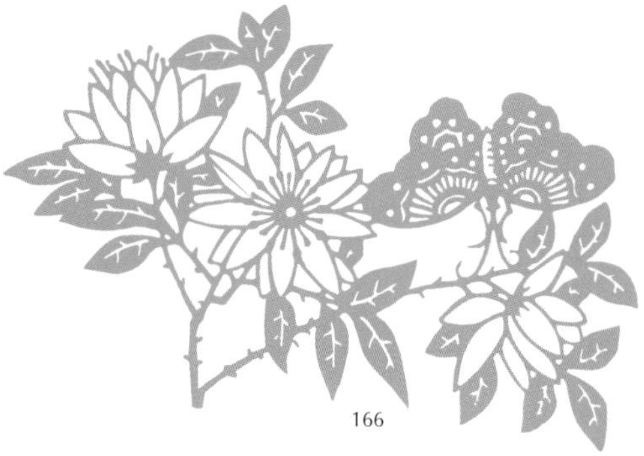

166

167

168

169

170

171

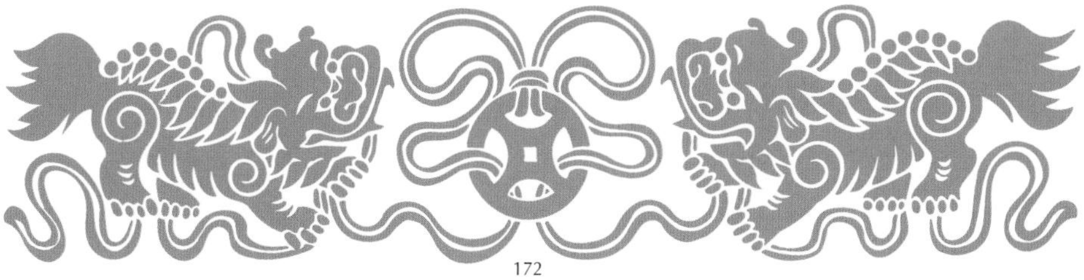
172

173

174

175

176

177

178

179

180

181

182

183

184

185

186

187

188

189

190

191

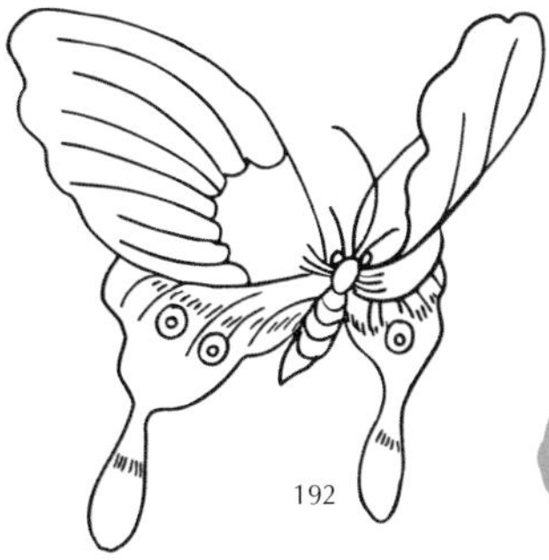

192

193

194

195

196

197

198

199

200

201

202

203

204

205

206

207

208

209

210

211

212

213

214

215

216

217

218

219

220

221

222

223

224

225

226

227

228

229

230

231

232

233

234

235

236

237

238

242

239

240

241

243

244

245

246

247

248

249

250

251

252

253

254

255

256

257

259

258

260

261

262

263

264

265

266

267

268

269

270

271

272

273

274

275

276

277

278

279

280

281

282

283

284

285

286

288

289

287

290

291

292

293

294

296

295

298

297

299

300